AF560843

Sri Aurobindo

The Spiritual Revolutionary

Published in 2002 by

Rupa & Co

7/16, Ansari Road, Daryaganj
New Delhi 110 002

Sales Centres:
Allahabad Bangalore Chandigarh Chennai
Dehradun Hyderabad Jaipur Kathmandu
Kolkata Ludhiana Mumbai Pune

Photographs courtesy: Sri Aurobindo Ashram Trust, Pondicherry

ISBN: 81-7167-866-1

Cover & Book Design by
Arrt Creations
45 Nehru Apts, Kalkaji, New Delhi 110 019
arrt@vsnl.com

Printed in India by
Gopsons Papers Ltd
A-14 Sector 60
Noida 201 301

Sri Aurobindo

The Spiritual Revolutionary

Atulindra Nath Chaturvedi

Rupa . Co

Dedicated to the memory of my Mother
And for my Father, fellow bibliomaniac

CONTENTS

"All Life is Yoga"

SRI AUROBINDO

India, in the late 19th and early 20th centuries, was fortunate enough to see the emergence of a remarkable number of exceptional individuals dedicated to the resurgence and revitalisation of the nation, in politics or the cultural and religious fields. Among them were Raja Rammohun Roy, Swami Dayanand, Swami Vivekananda, Rabindranath Tagore, Jawaharal Nehru, and, of course, Mahatma Gandhi.

However, none bridged the divide between the political and the spiritual as did the political activist Aurobindo Ghose, who blazed across the political firmament like a shooting star, and then, as the sage Sri Aurobindo, became the beacon whose light still draws millions. How the political pathfinder in a nation striving for liberation transformed himself into a rational mystic with a universal vision remains a continuing human puzzle.

Chapter One

The Making of a Revolutionary

Calcutta in the late 19th century was a unique city. It was not only the capital of British India; it was, clearly, the intellectual capital of India. The first intellectual ferment that resulted in the phenomenon known as the Indian Renaissance took place here. The city was saturated in the rediscovery of India's past, and the new, radical thoughts propounded by Raja Rammohun Roy, the Brahmo Samaj and Henry Derozio's iconoclastic ideas

It was in this city, that Aurobindo Ackroyd Ghose was born on

August 15, 1872. His mother, Swarnlata, was the daughter of Raj Narayan Bose, a Brahmo leader. His father, Dr Krishnadhan Ghose was a District Civil Surgeon in the service of the Government of Bengal. Ghose was an avowed anglophile, and refused to permit any Indian influence on his children. Aurobindo and his siblings learnt to speak English from their nurse, Miss Paget and some broken Hindustani from the butler. For the first five years of his life, Aurobindo could not speak a word of Bengali.

At the age of seven, Aurobindo and his brothers were uprooted and sent to live in England with Reverend Drewett and his

St. Paul's School, London (North Front, 1886)

Aurobindo as a young boy in England

wife in Manchester. Aurobindo later wrote that his father left strict instructions with the Drewetts that the boys "should not be allowed to make the acquaintance of any Indian or undergo any Indian influence". He also said that just before leaving for England, "I was lying down one day when I saw suddenly a great darkness rushing into me and enveloping me... After that I had a great *tamas*—darkness—always hanging on to me through my stay in England. It left me only when I was coming back to India."

In 1884, they moved to London, where Aurobindo entered the prestigious St. Paul's School. Aurobindo impressed the headmaster, Dr Walker, with his abilities, and was taken under his wings. He was given a thorough grounding in Greek, Latin, Italian and German. Aurobindo distinguished himself with his proficiency in the classics, literature and history. He developed an interest in poetry, especially Shelley's *The Revolt Of Islam,* and began to write verse himself—at first in Greek and Latin

All this took place in a situation of extreme poverty, as his father sent money in a very erratic manner. As Aurobindo recalled, "During this period Aurobindo used to get a slice or two of bread and butter and a cup of tea in the morning and in the evening a penny saveloy. For nearly two years, he had to go practically without dinner at that young age. He had no overcoat to protect him from the rigours of the London winter and there was no proper heating arrangement in the office where he slept, nor had he a proper bedroom."

Aurobindo lived here in Manchester

By the time he left St. Paul's, Aurobindo had won the Butterworth Prize for Literature and the Bedford Prize for History. In 1890, he secured an Open Scholarship for the classics at King's College at Cambridge. During his final year at St. Paul's, Aurobindo scored high marks in the Indian Civil Service examination (ICS), especially

obindo's room at Kings's Lane, Cambridge

in Greek and Latin, and he became a probationer, receiving a small stipend.

Aurobindo seems to have shouldered the double burden of studying the classics and preparing for the Civil Service with ease. He fared well in the First Part of the Tripos and also won several college prizes. However, he did not graduate as he had only two years at his disposal, instead of the four years required for qualifying for a degree.

At the same time, two other events took place that were to shape his life — politics and spirituality. His anglophile father soon began to detest the British regime, and sent his young son critical articles from *The Bengalee.* Aurobindo's interest in politics grew apace, and he spoke quite often, breathing fire and brimstone, at the Indian Majlis in Cambridge — an organisation of Indian students with a political bent. He also joined a secret society called The Lotus and Dagger, dedicated to driving the British from India. This, however, was a still-born affair.

At this time, Aurobindo had no special interest in religion, and described himself as an agnostic. During his studies for the civil services he came across an account of the six schools of Indian philosophy and was attracted by the description of the *atman* in *advaita*. He recalled, "It was borne in upon his mind that here might be a true clue to the reality behind life and the world." Thus came about Aurobindo's great spiritual awakening.

Aurobindo passed the final examinations for the ICS as well as the medical test, but failed — because he did not appear for the mandatory riding test. He was given four chances to appear, but did not turn up each time. Why did he throw everything that he had worked so hard for? Aurobindo explained: "I appeared for the ICS because my father wanted it and I was too young to understand. Later, I found out what sort of work it was and I had

King's Lane, Cambridge

Aurobindo Ghose in Baroda

disgust for administrative life and work. My interest was in poetry and study of language and in patriotic action."

What was Aurobindo now to do? Fate took a decisive hand in the person of Sir Sayajirao Gaekwar, the ruler of Baroda. After an interview in London, Gaekwar agreed to admit Aurobindo into the Baroda State Service. Aurobindo set sail for Bombay in January, 1893 on the *Carthage* and arrived on February 6. As he set foot again on Indian soil, Aurobindo was given the terrible news that his father was dead. Dr Ghose had been given the wrong information that his son had died on board the *Roumania,* and the shock killed him.

While in England, Aurobindo appears to have embarked upon certain spiritual exercises, but with little result. However, as he descended at Apollo Bunder, the first of his spiritual experiences occurred. Aurobindo writes: "Since I set foot on the Indian soil on the Apollo Bunder in Bombay, I began to have spiritual experiences, but these were not divorced from this world but had an inner and infinite bearing on it, such as a feeling of the Infinite pervading material space and the Immanent inhabiting material objects and bodies."

Aurobindo's great journey within had begun...

CHAPTER TWO

The Karamyogin

The princely states were by and large, poorly run, with their rulers more interested in amusing themselves. Baroda in the early 20th century was an exception to this rule. It was one of the best-administered princely states in India, and in the educational sphere, it was in some ways ahead of British India. The Gaekwar was an enlightened ruler, with an uncanny ability to recruit many an able person to man the Baroda State Service.

Aurobindo was first put to work in the Survey Department as a

Sir Sayajirao Gaekwar, The Maharaja of Baroda

trainee. He was then shifted first to the Revenue Department and then to the Secretariat. He then began teaching French at the Baroda College, before joining it as a professor of English. He went on become the Vice-Principal, and then Principal before he finally left Baroda in 1907.

The Gaekwar often called upon Aurobindo for help, due to his command of English. Aurobindo's exceptional report on the Bapat case impressed the Gaekwar greatly. The result was that Aurobindo was called upon to deal with the voluminous correspondence between Baroda and the Viceroy, Lord Curzon over a perceived insult. He also began to draft the ruler's letters and speeches.

It was a time when most rulers' speeches consisted of glowing praise for India's progress under the Raj. An Aurobindo-drafted speech made at the Ahmedabad Industrial Exhibition in 1902, therefore, was refreshing for its frankness regarding the downfall of indigenous industry, resulting in poverty.

The Gaekwar appointed Aurobindo as his secretary during a visit to Kashmir, but the association ended quickly. Aurobindo could not stand the constant demand on his time, and the ruler had little patience with Aurobindo's reluctance to wait on him hand and foot. Nevertheless, Aurobindo continued as an advisor.

It was during this visit to Kashmir that Aurobindo had another of his experiences, this time at the temple of Shankaracharya, which he later retold in his poem, *Adwaita*. More important, however, was the experience of a near-accident in Baroda, which he captured in a 1939 poem — *The Godhead*.

I sat behind the dance of Danger's hooves
In the shouting street that seemed a futurist's whim
And suddenly fell, exceeding Nature's grooves,
In me, enveloping me the body of Him.
Above my head a mighty head was seen,
A face with the calm of immortality
And an omnipotent gaze that held the scene
In the vast circle of its sovereignty.

At the Baroda College, Aurobindo became a highly respected, if somewhat eccentric, professor. Dismayed by the rigidity of the curriculum, and the fact that the only interest of students was to pass the examinations, he tried to find a via media. He forced students to work hard on their essays, making notations such as 'Fit for Standard III', 'How did you get into college' on those which failed to make the mark. He also made time for extra-curricular activities such as a student newspaper and debating society.

In 1901, Aurobindo made perhaps the only mistake of his life. He married Mrinalini Bose of Calcutta. While Aurobindo was in Baroda, the match worked. However, once his political activities gained pace, and he left for Calcutta, Mrinalini was left on her own. She died in 1918. Aurobindo wrote to his father-in-law: "I am afraid I shall never be good for much in the way of domestic virtues. I have tried, very ineffectively, to some part of my duty as…a husband, but there is something too strong in me which forces me to subordinate everything else to it."

Living a full life, Aurobindo had little time to himself. But what little there was, he threw into intense literary activity. He began to learn Bengali and Sanskrit, and make translations from Kalidasa, the *Mahabharata* and the *Ramayana*. He wrote poems, some of which were published in 1898 as *Songs To Myrtilla,* an essay on Bankim, and studied Hinduism in depth. He also began to practice yoga, though it was not until 1904 that he realised that it was possible for him to channelise his yogic exercises into political activity. As he wryly observed, his was "a side-door entry into the spiritual life."

Soon after his return to India, Aurobindo noted, "The patriot who offers advice to a great nation in an era of change and turmoil, should be very confident that he has something worth saying before he ventures to speak; but if he can really put some new aspect on a momentous question or emphasise any side of it that has not been clearly understood, it is his bounden duty, however obscure he may be, to ventilate it."

Khaserao Jadhav's bungalow, in Baroda, were Aurobindo lived

In 1906, with students of his English class at Baroda College

Aurobindo had something to say, and the time for it to be said came in 1893. D.G. Deshpande, a Cambridge friend, invited him to contribute to the English section of the English-Marathi magazine *Induprakash*. Aurobindo anonymously contributed a series of nine articles under the title *New Lamps For Old*.

They were scathing attacks on the Indian National Congress, a political party, then controlled by those who were later known as moderates. They wished to secure a measure of self-rule through constitutional means. This is a sample of what Aurobindo thought of them: "I say, of the Congress, then, this—that its aims are mistaken, that the spirit in which it proceeds towards their accomplishment is not a spirit of sincerity and whole-heartedness, and that the methods it has chosen are not the right methods, and the leaders in whom it trusts, not the right sort of men to be leaders; in brief, that we are at present the blind led, if not by the blind, at any rate by the one-eyed."

There was consternation in Congress circles. Justice Mahadev Govind Ranade, an eminent Congressman, told Deshpande that the magazine could be prosecuted for sedition. Aurobindo was told to tone down his articles. Ranade later asked to meet Aurobindo. He told him not to write such articles, but to engage

Baroda, January 1908

himself in other work for the Congress, like prison reform!

Aurobindo, instead, began to establish links with the more radical sections of the Congress — such as the Maratha leader Bal Gangadhar Tilak, whom he met at the 1902 Industrial Exhibition. He attended the 1905 session of the Congress and met its leaders. He also, with the help of his brother, Barin, planted the seeds of an underground revolutionary movement in Bengal. He established contact with revolutionaries such as P. Mitter, and established a Committee of Five consisting of Sister Nivedita (an associate of Swami Vivekananda), Satyendranath Tagore, P. Mitter, C.R. Das and Jatin, to oversee the growth of the movement. There were, however, differences between the members, and the goal of a revolutionary movement suffered.

Then, in an administrative blunder of major proportions. Lord Curzon divided the province of Bengal into two. This electrified the country, and galvanised the moribund political scene. Protests were held through the length and breadth of Bengal. The time, Aurobindo decided, to come out in the open had come. He left Baroda for Calcutta, never to resume service there again.

Chapter Three

The Prophet Of Nationalism

When Aurobindo arrived in Calcutta in March, 1906; the Swadeshi movement was rocking the province. Aurobindo had been present at the Benares session of the Congress, where a resolution calling for the boycott of foreign goods was passed. While most Congress leaders felt that boycott was legitimate only in the context of Bengal, Aurobindo felt that it was possible that a stronger leadership could well make it an all-India policy and strategy, and radicalise the Congress organisation.

Sylhet, September 1909

Aurobindo was already known in some sections as the author of a pamphlet titled *No Compromise*. The story goes that when the venerable Congress leader Surendranath Banerjea read it, he declared that it could have been written only by an Englishman. He was then informed of the identity of the author. At that, he reportedly exclaimed, "Oh, only Aurobindo could have written like this!"

Uttarpara, April 1908. Sri Aurobindo (far right), Bipin Chandra Pal (far left)

Shortly after his arrival in Calcutta, Aurobindo attended a meeting of the National Council of Education, which had set up the Bengal National College. The college was established to support those students who had joined the swadeshi movement, and as a consequence, been expelled from government-controlled institutions. Aurobindo took charge of the college on his 34th birthday, and taught English, French and history.

As the college was dominated by moderate elements, its curriculum was not radical enough for Aurobindo. Nevertheless, it is interesting to note what he had to say about the nature of education: "We may describe national education tentatively as the education which

Bande Mataram

Weekly Edition.

PUBLISHED EVERY SUNDAY.

Price One Anna. Price One Anna.

VOL. I. | CALCUTTA, SUNDAY, SEPTEMBER 29, 1907. | NO. 18.

OUR PICTURE GALLERY.

SJT. AUROBINDO GHOSE.

Calcutta, September 1907. Front page of Bande Mataram, after Aurobindo's acquittal in the Bande Mataram Sedition Trial

starting with the past and making full use of the present, builds up a great nation. Whoever wishes to cut off the nation from its past is no friend of our national growth. Whoever fails to take advantage of the present is losing us the battle of life. We must therefore save for India all that she has stored up of knowledge, character and noble thought in her immemorial past. We must acquire for her the best knowledge that Europe can give her and assimilate it to her own peculiar type of national temperament."

Aurobindo also took part in the Barisal conference of the Bengal Provincial Congress, in the company of the moderate Banerjee, the radical Bipin Chandra Pal, and the equivocal Motilal Ghose. The meeting took place in defiance of a ban. After the leaders entered the pavilion, shouting *Bande Mataram,* a nationalist slogan, the police attacked the rank and file. A contemporary observer, Bhupendranath Basu observed: "I recall that while all others were excited, Sri Aurobindo was unperturbed; he was satisfied with the evolution of thought and activity precipitated at Barisal."

While the moderates controlled the nationalist papers, the radicals—who called themselves the Nationalist Party—had recourse only to the Bengali *Yugantar,* for which Aurobindo began to write. Soon after, an English journal was started, *Bande Mataram.* Aurobindo agreed to write a daily piece for the paper, and quickly took control

After taking over as Principal of Bengal National College, Calcutta, August 1907

of it. It was the most radical paper, not only in Bengal, but the whole of India, and was, for some time, possibly the most widely-read paper of its kind in the country. Aurobindo's command of English, and his careful marshalling of facts and argument won him admirers even among his British foes.

Aurobindo presiding over a meeting at Surat, December 1907. Lokmanya Tilak is addressing the gathering

Most importantly, Aurobindo was the first to declare that *swaraj* was not just self-rule under the British, but full and complete independence from the colonial power. He published a series of articles on passive resistance, another on the political philosophy of revolution, and many leaders on the pressing questions of the day.

With Nationalist leaders at Surat, December 1907, (From left—front row) Ganesh Srikrishna Khaparde, Ashwini Kumar Dutt; (middle row) Sardar Ajitsingh, Aurobindo, Lokmanya Tilak, Saiyad Haider Reza; (back row) Dr. Munjee, Ramaswamy, K. Kuverji Desai

The moderates, however, continued to dominate the Congress organisation, though the extremists had popular support. The sharp differences between the two culminated in a split in the party at the Congress session at Surat in 1906, with each wing going its separate way. Late in life, Aurobindo revealed in a letter that he was the person responsible for the actual events that led to the split, taking the help of some Maratha strongmen to break up the session by creating chaos. Though there were attempts to reunite the two factions, in the end, it was the extremist programme which was to be the charter of the Congress in the future

Simultaneously, Aurobindo continued his yogic exercises. He met a famous spiritual master, Swami Brahamanand, and then was taken by his brother, Barin, to meet Lele a Maharashtrian yogi, in 1907. Aurobindo recalled: "He was giving me detailed instructions. In the meantime I told him of a mantra that had arisen in my heart. Suddenly while giving instructions he stopped and asked me if I could rely absolutely on Him who gave

The emblem of Yugantar

At Uttarpara, April 1908

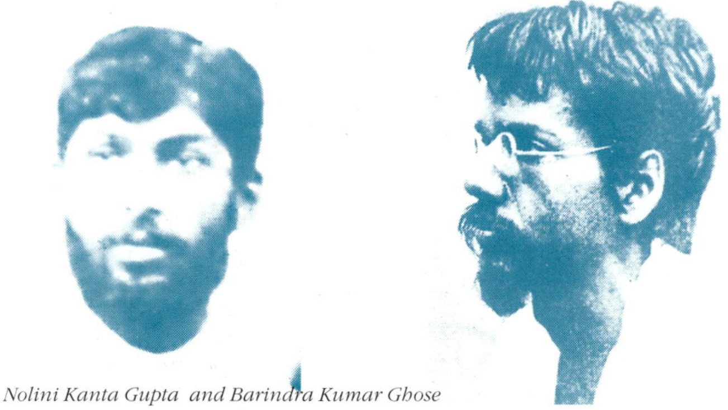

Nolini Kanta Gupta and Barindra Kumar Ghose

me the mantra. I replied that I could always do that. Then Lele said there was no need for further instructions."

Aurobindo had to speak on nationalism at Girgaum, but felt he could not do so in this present condition. Lele told him not to worry, but to greet the audience as *Narayana* (God), and then a voice would speak. This is exactly what happened: "You call yourselves Nationalists. What is Nationalism? Nationalism is not a mere political programme; Nationalism is a religion that has come from God; Nationalism is a creed which you shall have to live. Let no man dare to call himself a Nationalist if he does so merely with a sort of intellectual pride, thinking that he is more patriotic, thinking that he is something higher than those who do not call themselves

Khudiram Bose and Prafulla Chaki

by that name. If you are going to be a Nationalist...you must do it in the religious spirit."

The revolutionary movement had gained momentum in Bengal. After Prafulla Chaki and Khudiram Bose injured two Englishwomen traveling in a carriage in Muzaffarpur that belonged Kingsford, an ICS officer, Aurobindo and 25 others, including Barin, and Nolini Kanta Gupta, were arrested on May 2, 1908. They were charged with waging war against the King, the penalty for which was death.

The Alipore Bomb case was the first revolutionary conspiracy case in India. The judge, ironically, was C.P. Beachcroft, who had been beaten by Aurobindo at Cambridge in Greek—and who had bested him in Bengali! The brilliant barrister Eardley Norton was lured

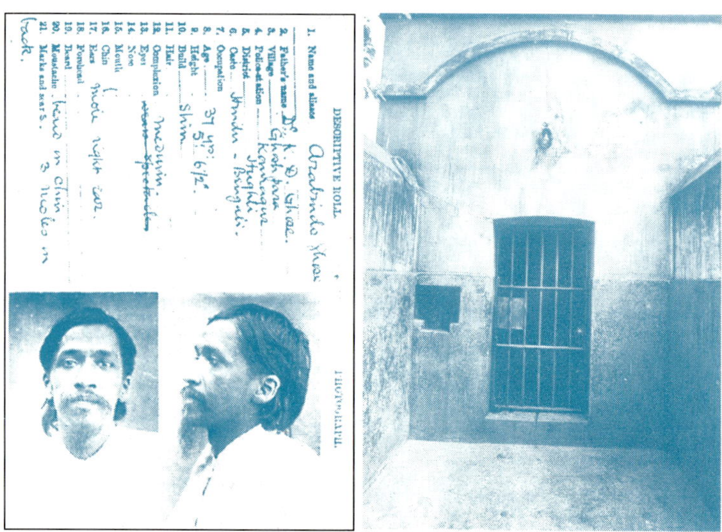
DESCRIPTIVE ROLL

1. Name and aliases Arabindo Ghose
2. Father's name Dr. K. D. Ghose.
3. Village Ghoshpara
4. Police-station Konnagore
5. District Hughli
6. Caste Hindu - Bengali.
7. Occupation
8. Age 37 yrs.
9. Height 5' 6½"
10. Build Slim
11. Hair
12. Complexion medium
13. Eyes
14. Nose
15. Mouth
16. Chin
17. Ears mole right ear.
18. Forehead
19. Beard
20. Moustache
21. Marks and scars. mole on chin 3 moles in back.

PHOTOGRAPH.

Aurobindo's identity card at Alipore Jail, Calcutta and his solitary cell

from Madras to prosecute the case. The young Chittaranjan Das represented Aurobindo. Das' defense plea was masterly: "Long after this controversy is hushed in silence, long after this turmoil ceases, long after he is dead and gone, he will be looked upon as the prophet of patriotism, as the prophet of nationalism and the lover of humanity. Long after he is dead and gone, his words will be echoed and re-echoed not only in India, but across seas and lands." On May 6, 1909, Aurobindo was acquitted.

Arbind Mandir ('The Temple of Aurobindo') A poster printed in the 1930s showing Sri Aurobindo surrounded by revolutionary heroes such as Bhagat Singh

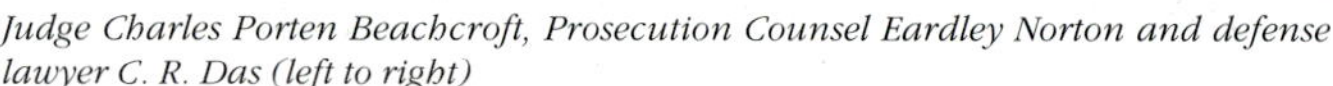

Judge Charles Porten Beachcroft, Prosecution Counsel Eardley Norton and defense lawyer C. R. Das (left to right)

During his year-long incarceration, Aurobindo's spiritual experiences reached a climax. He had a vision of the Divine as Krishna in the form of Vasudeva, "as all beings and all that is". This vision of the Divine was accompanied by a deepening of Aurobindo's individual awareness into what he called "cosmic consciousness". He described his experiences in a speech at Uttarpara, and in a later memoir.

On release, Aurobindo reverted to form. He began to publish a weekly, *Karamyogin* in English, and *Dharma,* in Bengali. However, in mid-February, 1910 he was told that there was a move to arrest and deport him from India. At this point, he received an *adesh* (order) from an inner voice, which told him that his political work was over, that freedom for India was assured, and that greater work awaited him. The voice told him to leave Calcutta, and go to the French enclave of Chandernagore. Another *adesh* told him to proceed from there to Pondicherry, another French enclave, near Madras.

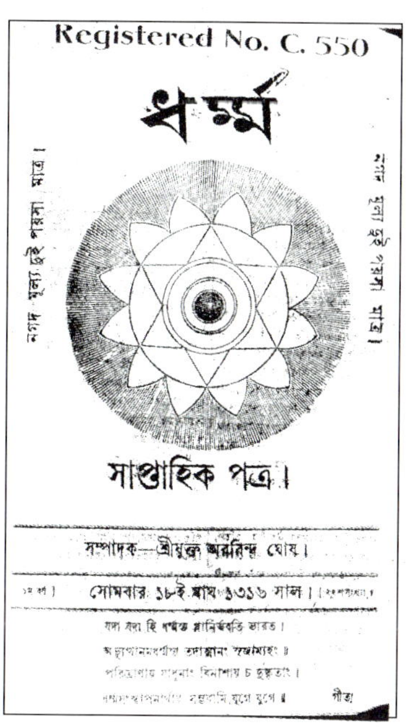

Registered No. C. 550

ধর্ম্ম

নগদ মূল্য দুই পয়সা মাত্র।

নগদ মূল্য দুই পয়সা মাত্র।

সাপ্তাহিক পত্র।

সম্পাদক—শ্রীযুক্ত অরবিন্দ ঘোষ।

১ম বর্ষ] সোমবার ১৮ই মাঘ ১৩১৬ সাল।

যদা যদা হি ধর্ম্মস্য গ্লানির্ভবতি ভারত।
অভ্যুত্থানমধর্ম্মস্য তদাত্মানং সৃজাম্যহং॥
পরিত্রাণায় সাধূনাং বিনাশায় চ দুষ্কৃতাং।
ধর্ম্মসংস্থাপনার্থায় সম্ভবামি যুগে যুগে॥ গীতা

Front page of Dharma, *a Bengali weekly edited by Aurobindo in 1909-10*

On the night of March 31, Aurobindo, accompanied by Bijoy Nag, boarded a ship and left Calcutta. As Calcutta faded away into the darkness, it closed the chapter on Aurobindo's political life and opened one on the extraordinary adventure of consciousness he was engaged in.

Chapter Four

The Early Years in Pondicherry

Pondicherry, in the early 20th century was a sleepy town living on its past glory. Small, picturesque, it is not really different today from what it must have been then. The importance of Pondicherry lies in the fact that it was a safe haven for refugees from British oppression. The most notable exiles were a small group of nationalists grouped around the fiery poet Subramania Bharati, who brought out the Tamil paper *India*.

When Sri Aurobindo (as we shall now call him) sailed into the small harbour on April 4, 1910, never to leave the town again, it was this group, led by Bharati, which formed his welcome committee. He was taken immediately to the house of Shankara Chettair, a nationalist sympathiser, and there lived in near seclusion and poverty for almost six months. Though he left it up to God to provide for him, Sri Aurobindo once observed, "No doubt, God will provide, but He has contracted a habit of waiting till the last moment!"

After the case against the *Karamyogin* was dismissed, Sri Aurobindo wrote to the *Hindu* in Madras. He announced his presence in Pondicherry, and that

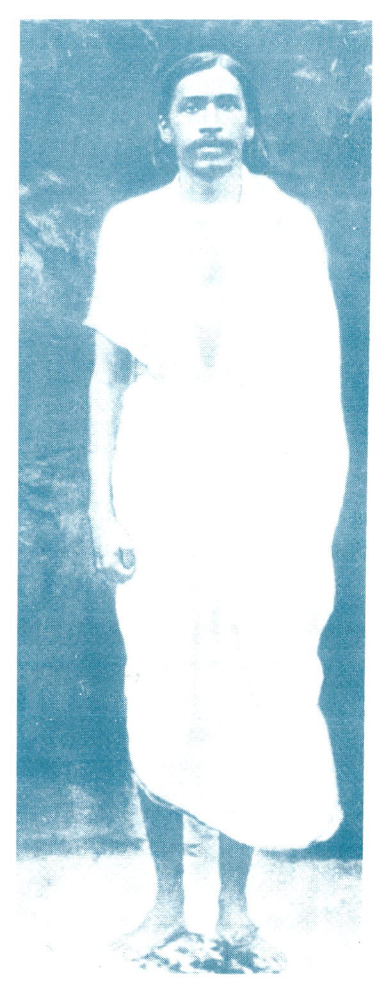

Sri Aurobindo at Pondicherry, August 1911

Sri Aurobindo in Pondicherry, around 1918

he was living as a "religious recluse" and that he wished to see and correspond with no one in connection with political subjects. Sri Aurobindo's wish was in vain. He again wrote the *Hindu* in 1911, "I find myself besieged by devotees who insist on seeing me whether I will or not. They have crossed all India to see me... They only wish to stand at a distance and get *mukti* by gazing on my face... I wish to inform all future pilgrims that their journey will be in vain."

Sri Aurobindo at first tried to keep his presence secret from the British. However, he discovered that they were not so ready to let go of their prey. A local politician was hired to kidnap and take him to British India. However, the plot did not materialise. There was yet another attempt to prejudice the local police against Sri

Aurobindo. Some revolutionary pamphlets were thrown into a well at Chettiar's house with the aim that they should be discovered by the police, who would then take action against these dangerous people.

REGISTERED NO. C532.

SUBSCRIPTION RUPEES 5.

KARMAYOGIN

A WEEKLY REVIEW

OF

National Religion, Literature, Science, Philosophy, &c.,

Vol. I. | SATURDAY 6th NOVEMBER 1909.

Front page of Karmayogin, *an English weekly edited by Aurobindo in 1909-10*

However, the pamphlets were discovered and Sri Aurobindo immediately called in the police himself. The French officer looked at Sri Aurobindo's books exclaimed, "He knows Greek! He knows Latin! He is a scholar!" and called off the search. He then invited Sri Aurobindo to visit him, which he duly did.

A singular meeting took place in 1910, which was to have a deep impact on Sri Aurobindo's life. A French politician and spiritualist, Paul Richard, visited him. He went away convinced that Sri Aurobindo was the person that he and his wife, Mirra, had been looking for in their spiritual search. The Richards duly came in 1914. Mirra recorded this of her first meeting with Sri Aurobindo, "As soon as I saw A.G. I recognised him as the well-known being known as Krishna and this is enough to explain why I am fully convinced that my place and work are near him, in India." The Richards proposed that they bring out a journal dedicated to a synthesis of yoga and the knowledge that Sri Aurobindo was acquiring. It was to be jointly edited by all three. The name of the journal was to be *Arya*. The first issue appeared on August 15, 1914, Sri Aurobindo's 42nd birthday. Its purpose was clearly enunciated: "Its object to feel out for the thought of the future, to help in shaping its foundations and to link it to the best and most vital thought of the past."

However, the forced departure of the Richards at the outbreak of the First World War laid the burden of bringing out the *Arya* on the shoulders of Sri Aurobindo, who discontinued it in 1920, though by then it had become a paying proposition. Sri Aurobindo wrote all the material for the 64-page journal, typed it, and proof-read it every month. It is in the *Arya* that Sri Aurobindo wrote all the works that are the basis for his reputation as a philosopher, Sanskrit scholar, political scientist, and literary critic. *The Synthesis Of Yoga, The Life Divine, Defence Of Indian Culture, The Human Cycle,*

Sri Aurobindo Ashram, Pondicherry

translations from the *Upanishads* etc, appeared here for the first time

Mirra Richard, The Mother

Sri Aurobindo's yogic experiments took on a new dimension in Pondicherry. We are fortunate that he kept a record of these experiments. They are stunning in showing that internally, spiritually, Sri Aurobindo was constantly evolving, at the same time that he was carrying on a varied and hectic external life. And if anybody thought that spirituality is an easy and painless task, a reading of the record should disabuse him. The development of Sri Aurobindo's Integral Yoga will be discussed in the next chapter.

Mirra returned to Pondicherry in April, 1920. Six years later, Sri Aurobindo put her in charge of the material and spiritual aspects of the Sri Aurobindo Ashram on its founding. He began to call her The Mother at this time. He looked upon her not as a disciple, but as his spiritual equal and collaborator. She continued her work until her death at the age of ninety-five in 1973.

The Ashram was formally established in 1926, though Sri Aurobindo felt uneasy about the name. The formalisation of the working arrangements was necessitated by the increase in the number of inmates, who had grown in number from only a handful to about 400.

The event of November 24, 1926, was the most momentous after the coming of The Mother. On this day, according to Sri Aurobindo, his yogic exercises were able to bring down the Overmind to Earth. Sri Aurobindo now began to withdraw from the disciples around him, seeing them only occasionally. He retained contact with them through letters, notes, and The Mother. He also saw fewer visitors, though a select few were able to meet him. Over the years, they included Rabindranath Tagore, C.R. Das, and the French explorer Alexandra David-Neel.

Several attempts were also made to draw Sri Aurobindo back into the political fray. About ten years after he reached Pondicherry, Dr Joseph Baptista invited him to take charge of a newspaper to be brought out on behalf of a new nationalist party that Bal Gangadhar Tilak and others were planning to set up. He rejected the offer, saying that, "Pondicherry is my place of retreat, my cave of *tapsya,* not of the ascetic kind, but of a brand of my own invention. I must finish that, I must be internally armed and equipped for my work before I leave it." He added, "My line and intention of political activity would differ considerably from anything now current in the field." Similarly, when Dr Munje invited him to become the President of the Congress he replied firmly that, "I am no longer first and foremost a politician, but have definitely commenced another kind of work with a spiritual basis..."

Though Sri Aurobindo had withdrawn from the political field, he still maintained contact with those who were active, and kept himself abreast of the latest development, and was never reluctant to discuss them in private talks at the Ashram. But it was all secondary to the pursuit of his spiritual goals.

Chapter Five

Sri Aurobindo's Integral Yoga

Before we discuss Sri Aurobindo's concept of Integral Yoga, it is necessary to emphasise and remember a few things: Aurobindo was a poet before he became a politician; his political and yoga experimentations were not exclusive to each other, but intertwined; his yoga did not arise from philosophical speculation, his philosophy — as set out in *The Life Divine* and *The Synthesis Of Yoga* — was the result of his experiments in what he described as integral yoga.

Another point to note is that the underlying motif of Sri Aurobindo's life and thought is the concept of evolution, as he once pointed out while discussing an essay, *Bases Of Yoga*. It contained his early ideas on yoga, and he developed them further. Sri Aurobindo's ideas — political or spiritual — were never static; they were always in a constant state of evolution.

Before we briefly discuss Sri Aurobindo's yoga and philosophy, it will be interesting to note a few subtle aspects of his life and thought. When he formalised the Ashram in 1926, he made a very pointed statement on its character, "This Ashram has been created with another object than that ordinarily common to such institutions, not for renunciation of the world but as a center and field of practice for the evolution of another kind and form of life." Again, in 1932 he wrote, "This is not an Ashram like others — the members are not *sanyasins*; it is not *moksha* that is the sole aim of the yoga here. What is being done here is a preparation for a work — a work which will be founded on yogic consciousness, and can have no other foundation."

Also, Sri Aurobindo never set up a formal *guru-shisya* (teacher-student) relationship that is typical of ashrams in India. Those who gathered around him and The Mother were described as *sadhaks* (aspirants, seekers). Sri Aurobindo eschewed the formality that characterised the *guru-shisya* tradition. Once, when he acceded to a *sadhak's* desire to mediate in his presence, he sat in a chair reading a newspaper. And a strange guru it was who politely asked permission to enter one's room, or said excuse me when his foot accidentally touched another's. Once, he wistfully told the *sadhaks* that they never allowed him to come down to their level.

Sri Aurobindo arrived at Integral Yoga as a result of his intensive yogic meditations. It appears that these experiments never ceased, and continued till the end. Integral Yoga is 'integral' in the sense that it integrates the existing methods of yoga, yet, it transcends the goals and essential principles of the traditional Indian systems of yoga. As Sri Aurobindo wrote, "On the whole, for an Integral Yoga the special methods of *Rajayoga* and *Hathayoga* may be useful at time in certain stages of the process, but are not indispensable. It is true that their principal aims must be included in the integrality of the Yoga; but they can be brought about by other means. For the methods of the Integral Yoga must be mainly spiritual and dependence on physical methods or fixed psychic or psychophysical processes on a large scale would be the substitution of a lower for a higher action."

The Mother

Integral Yoga is integral since it includes *jnanayoga*, which "aims at the realisation of the unique and supreme Self by the method of intellectual reflection, *vicara*, to right discrimination, *viveka*", *bhaktiyoga*, which "aims at the enjoyment of the Supreme Lord and Bliss and normally utilises the conception of the Supreme Lord"; and *karamyoga*, "which aims at the dedication of every human activity to the Supreme Will."

Integral Yoga attempts to synthesise these three yoga systems by a "central principle common to all, which will include and utilise in the right place and proportion their particular principles." The principle that includes and transforms these three yogas is the Yoga of Self-Perfection. Sri Aurobindo summaries it thus: "The object of our synthetic Yoga must be more integral and comprehensive, embrace all these elements or these tendencies of a larger impulse of self-perfection and harmonise them or rather unify, and in order to do that successfully it must seize on a truth that is wider than the ordinary religious and higher than the mundane principle."

An interesting sidelight on Integral Yoga is that Sri Aurobindo did not give any method for it. As he wrote in a letter: "The way of yoga must be a living thing, not a mental principle or a set method to be stuck to against all necessary variations."

But what is the aim of this yoga? Sri Aurobindo informs us that, "A spiritual evolution, an evolution of consciousness in Matter is a constant developing self-formation till the form can reveal the indwelling spirit, is then the keynote, the central significant motive of the terrestrial existence." Nolini Kanta Gupta, who accompanied Sri Aurobindo into exile, notes "Sri Aurobindo's message is very simple, almost self-evident. The sum and substance of all he says is that man is growing and has to grow in consciousness, till he reaches the complete and perfect consciousness, not only in his individual but in his collective, that is to say, social life. In fact, the growth of consciousness is the supreme secret of life, the master key to earthly existence."

It is this growth of consciousness, that will put the seal and bring the divine life on earth. Till now, Matter and Spirit had been treated as two separate entities. In the eyes of Sri Aurobindo, this divide needs to be bridged: "The affirmation of a divine life upon earth and an immortal sense in mortal existence can have no base unless we recognise not only eternal Spirit as the inhabitant of the bodily mansion, the wearer of this mutable robe, but accept Matter of which it is made as a fit and noble material out of which He weaves constantly His garbs, builds recurrently the unending series of His mansions."

Chapter Six

The Last Years

Sri Aurobindo's seclusion continued into the 1930s, but came to an abrupt end on November 24, 1938. He fell down the stairs, and broke his right hip. This required constant medical attention. Since some of the Ashram inmates had some medical knowledge, so they and some outside doctors were in constant touch with Sri Aurobindo.

During the 1920s and 1930s, Sri Aurobindo spent a lot of time on

Sri Aurobindo, April 1950 (This photograph was taken by Henri-Cartier Bresson)

his correspondence. Thousands of letters were written on his yoga and other topics to seekers. Selections from the letters relating specifically to yoga have been published in the three-volume *Letters On Yoga*. However, after his accident, Aurobindo began to dictate his letters to a secretary, Nirodbaran.

Sri Aurobindo also resumed his evening talks, which were recorded by Nirodbaran and A.B. Purani. These range not only over yoga and the events of the day, but, for the first time, Sri Aurobindo was also drawn into reminiscences about his life, which are of immense value to any biographer. He also pointed out errors of fact or interpretation in the biographies which had begun to come out.

A return to literary activity also took place. Sri Aurobindo began to revise his writings from the *Arya*, and bring them out in book form. The first volume of *The Life Divine* came out in 1939, while the second, completely revised and expanded, was published the next year. The first part of *The Synthesis Of Yoga* was published in 1948, while *The Human Cycle* and *The Ideal Of Human Unity*, his most complete social writings, were published in 1949 and 1950.

Sri Aurobindo also returned to his first love. He again started to write poems, which referred to his spiritual experiences, or, as in some cases, to the turbulent events that were taking place. *The*

Children Of Wotan written in August, 1940, clearly referred to the dangers of the advance of Hitler's forces in Europe:

Our leader is master of Fate, medium of her mysteries.

We have made the mind a cipher, we have strangled Thought with a cord;

Dead are now pity and honour, strength only is Nature's lord.

We build a new world-order,

We are the human Titans, the supermen dreamed by the sage.

A cross of the beast and demoniac with the godhead of power and will,

We are born in humanity's sunset, to the Night is our pilgrimage.

On the bodies of perishing nation, mid the cry of the cataclysms coming,

To the presto of bomb and shell and the aeroplanes' fatal humming,

We march, lit by Truth death-pyre, to the worlds's satanic age.

But most of his poetic work was devoted to completing *Savitri*, an epic poem which he began in the Baroda days but never finished. He dictated it line-by-line to Nirodbaran, who would then read it back to Sri Aurobindo. Further changes would then be made. In its final form, *Savitri* consisted of over 24,000 lines. From a straightforward retelling of the legend of Savitri and Satyavan, of love conquering death, Sri Aurobindo transformed the poem into an account of the possibilities of yoga in action, informed by his own experiences.

The power of the poetry and the scale of Sri Aurobindo's achievement can be gauged from this brief sample:

> *A marvelous sun looked down from ecstasy's skies*
> *On worlds of deathless bliss, perfection's home,*
> *Magical unfoldings of the Eternal's smile*
> *Capturing his secret heartbeats of delight.*
> *God's everlasting day surrounded her,*
> *Domains appeared of sempiternal light*
> *Invading all Nature with the Absolute's joy.*
> *Her body quivered with Eternity's touch.*

Her soul stood close to the founts of the infinite.
Infinity's finite fronts she lived in, new
For ever to an everlasting sight...
There lightning-filled with glory and with flame,
Melting in waves of sympathy and sight,
Smitten like a lyre that throbs to others' bliss,
Drawn by the cords of ecstasies unknown.
Her human nature faint with heaven's delight,
She beheld the clasp to earth denied and bore
The imperishable eyes of veilless love.

On the outbreak of war, Sri Aurobindo made his first public statement on politics in almost twenty years — in support of the allied cause against Hitler. This shocked public opinion in India. Many people were unable to understand how someone who had fought ardently against the British could now support them. But Sri Aurobindo was clear, Hitler represented a danger to India. If he won, then India would not become free, but suffer an even worse tyranny.

In a message to the Governor of Madras in 1940, he wrote, "We feel that not only is this a battle waged in just self-defence and in defence of the nations threatened with the world-domination of Germany and the Nazi system of life, but that it is a defence of civilisation and that of its highest attained social, cultural and spiritual values and of the whole future of humanity."

The British Government, realising that it needed the full support of Indians to fight the Japanese, in March, 1942, offered dominion status during the war, with independence to follow after victory. The Congress rejected the offer made by Sir Stafford Cripps, though Sri Aurobindo privately, through intermediaries, urged the Congress to accept it. Sri Aurobindo then publicly came out in support of the proposals, in a message to Cripps. He wrote: "As one who has been a nationalist leader and worker for India's independence... I wish to express my appreciation to you...I welcome it as an opportunity given to India to determine for herself, and organise in all liberty of choice, her freedom and unity, and take an effective 'place among the world's free nations. I hope that it will be accepted...I offer my public adhesion..."

Sri Aurobindo's next public message came on the occasion of Indian Independence in 1947. By a strange coincidence (though Sri

Aurobindo did not believe that it was coincidental) the freedom that he had predicted for his country almost 40 years ago, came on his 74th birthday. In his message, Sri Aurobindo spoke of the five dreams he had about the future of India and the world. The full text can be read in the appendix.

In 1948, Sri Aurobindo was the recipent of the Sir Cattamanchi Ramalinga Reddy National Prize, presented by Andhra University. In 1950, the Asiatic Society gave him an award. A concerted effort was also made by Aldous Huxley, Pearl Buck and others to nominate him for the Nobel Prize for literature.

Sri Aurobindo also relaxed his rules regarding outside visitors. In September, 1947, Maurice Schumann, a French diplomat and Francois Bacon, the Governor of French India, met him in connection with an Indo-French cultural institution they wished to set up in Pondicherry under his guidance. He also met K.M. Munshi, a minister in the Indian Government, and once a student of his at Baroda. Munshi was struck by his appearance, "I saw before me, a being completely transformed, radiant, blissful, enveloped in an atmosphere of god-like charm. He spoke in a low, clear voice, which stirred the depths of my being."

Sri Aurobindo's health began to decline, and he slipped in and out of coma, seemingly at will. On December 5, 1950, he went into *mahasamadhi*. His body was laid to rest in the grounds of the *ashram* on December 9, 1950.

The great adventure was over.

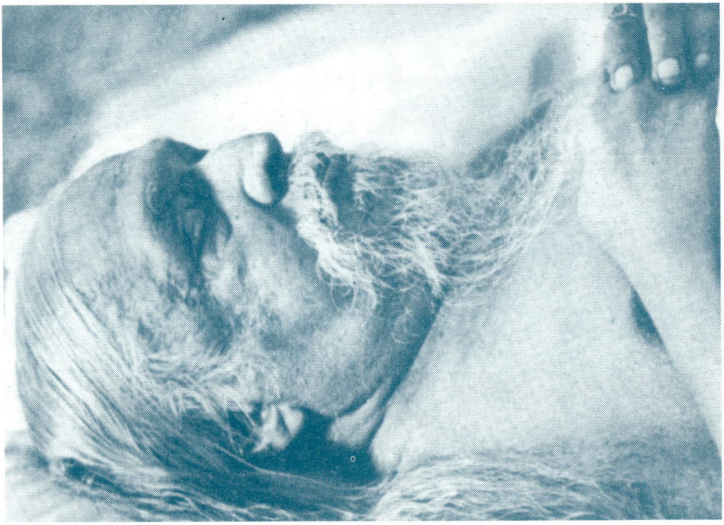

The India Independence Message, 1947

The following is the text of a message given by Sri Aurobindo on the occasion of India's Independence.

August 15, 1947 is the birthday of Free India. It marks for her the end of an old era, the beginnings of a new age. But it has a significance not only for us, but for Asia and the whole world; for it signifies the entry into the comity of nations of a new power with untold potentialities which has a great role to play in determining the political, social, cultural and spiritual future of humanity. To me personally, it must naturally be gratifying that this date, which was notable only for me because it was my own birthday celebrated by those who have accepted my gospel of life, should have acquired this vast significance. As a mystic, I take this identification, not as a fortuitous accident, but as a sanction and seal of the Divine Power which guides my steps on the work with which I began life. Indeed almost all the world movements which

I hoped to see fulfilled in my lifetime, though at that time they looked like impossible dreams, I can observe on this day either approaching fruition or initiated and on the way to their achievement.

I have been asked for a message on this great occasion, but I am perhaps hardly in a position to give one. All I can do is to make a personal declaration of the aims and ideals conceived in my childhood and youth and now watched in their beginning of fulfillment, because they are relevant to the freedom of India, since they are a part of what I believe to be India's future work, something in which she cannot but take a leading position. For I have always held and said that India was arising, not to serve her own material interests only, to achieve expansion, greatness, power, and prosperity — though these too she must not neglect — and certainly not like others to acquire domination of other peoples, but to live also for God and world as helper and leader of the whole human race. Those aims and ideals were in their natural order, that is, a revolution which would achieve India's freedom and her unity, the resurgence and liberation of Asia and her return to the great role which she had played in the progress of human civilisation; the rise of a new, a greater, brighter and nobler life for mankind which for its entire realisation would rest outwardly on an international unification of the separate existence of the peoples, preserving and securing their national life but drawing them together into an overriding and consumating oneness; the gift by India of her spiritual knowledge and her means for the spiritualisation of life to whole human race. Finally, a new step in the evolution which, by uplifting the consciousness to a higher level, would begin the solution of the many problems of existence which have perplexed and vexed humanity, since men began to think and to dream of individual perfection and a perfect society.

India is free, but she has not achieved unity, only a fissured and broken freedom. At one time, it almost seemed as if she might relapse into the chaos of separate States which preceded the British conquest. Fortunately, there has now developed a strong possibility that this disastrous relapse will be avoided. The wisely drastic policy of the Constituent Assembly makes it possible that the problem of the depressed classes will be solved without schism and fissure. But the old communal division into Hindu and Muslim seems to have hardened into the figure of a permanent political division of the country. It is to be hoped that the Congress and the nation will not accept the settled fact as for ever settled or as anything more than a temporary expedient. For if it lasts, India may be seriously weakened, even crippled; civil strife may remain always possible, possibly even a new invasion and foreign conquest. The partition of the country must go, it is to be hoped by a slackening of tension, by a progressive understanding of the need for peace and concord, by the constant necessity of common and concerted action, even of an instrument of union for that purpose. In this way unity may come about under whatever form — the exact form may have a pragmatic but not a fundamental importance. But by whatever means, the division must and will go. For without it the destiny of India might be seriously impaired and even frustrated. But that must not be.

Asia has arisen and large parts of it have been liberated or are at this moment being liberated; its other still subject parts are moving through whatever struggles towards freedom. Only a little has to be done and that will be done today or tomorrow. There India has her part to play and has begun to play it with an energy and ability which already indicates the measure of her possibilities and the place which she can take in the council of nations.

The unification of mankind is underway, though only in an imperfect initiative, organised but struggling against tremendous difficulties. But the momentum is there, and if the experience of history can be taken as a guide, it must inevitably increase until it conquers. Here too, India has begun to play a prominent part and, if she can develop that larger statesmanship which is not limited by the present facts and immediate possibilities but looks into the future and brings it nearer, her presence may make all the difference between a slow and timid and a bold and swift development. A catastrophe may intervene and interrupt or destroy what is being done, but even then the final result is sure. For in any case, the unification is a necessity in the course of Nature, an inevitable movement and its achievement can be safely foretold. Its necessity for the nations also is clear, for without it the freedom of the small peoples can never be safe hereafter, and even large and powerful nations cannot really be secure. India, if she remains divided, will not herself be sure of her safety. It is therefore to the interest of all that union should take place. Only human imbecility and stupid selfishness could prevent it. Against that, it has been said, even the Gods strive in vain; but it cannot stand forever against the necessity of Nature and the Divine Will. Nationalism will then have fulfilled itself; and international spirit and outlook must grow up and international forms and institutions; even it may be such developments as dual or multilateral citizenship and a voluntary fusion of cultures may appear in the process of the change and the spirit of nationalism losing its militancy may find things perfectly compatible with the integrity of its own outlook. A new spirit of oneness will take hold of the human race.

The spiritual gift of India to the world has already begun. India's spirituality is entering Europe and America in an ever increasing measure. The movement will grow; amid the disasters of the time, more and more eyes are turning towards her with hope and there is even increasing resort to not only her teachings, but to her psychic and spiritual practice. The rest is still a personal hope and an idea and ideal which has begun to take hold both in India and the West on forward-looking minds. The difficulties in the way are more formidable than in any other field of endeavour, but difficulties were made to be overcome and if the Supreme Will is there, they will be overcome. Here too, if this evolution is to take place, since it must come through a growth of the spirit and inner consciousness, the initiative can come from India and although the scope must be universal, the central movement may be hers.

Such is the content which I put into this date of India's liberation; whether or how soon this connection will be fulfilled, depends upon this new and free India.

Sri Aurobindo

Rabindranath Tagore's Poem to Sri Aurobindo

The following is the translation by Kshitish Chandra Sen and Dilip Kumar Roy of the poem 'Salutation' written by Rabindranath Tagore in 1907, after Sri Aurobindo's arrest.

Rabindranath, O Aurobindo, bows to thee!

O friend, my country's friend. O voice Incarnate, free

Of India's soil! — No soft renown has ever crowned thy lot;

Nor pelf nor careless comfort was for thee; thou hast sought
No petty bounty's boon, thc bcggar's dismal bowl
Thou never hast extended. For thy wakeful soul
Aspired to heights of bondless full perfection's birth,
For which all day and night the God in man on earth
Divinely strives — the glory which with solemn voice
The poet sings in high-winged rhythms — for which rejoice
Stout hearts to march on perilous paths — before whose flame
Of danger ease bows down its head in humble shame
And death forgets to fear.

When I behold thy face 'mid-bondage', pain and wrong
And black indignities, I hear the soul's great song
Of rapture unconfirmed, the chant the pilgrim sings
In which exultant Hope's immortal music rings,
O calm and solemn voice, voice heart-consoling, grand

And imperturbable, the Spirit of Bharat-land,
O pet, has placed upon thy face her eyes afire
With love and struck vast chords upon her vibrant lyre,
Wherein there is no voice of sorrow, shame or fear
Nor penury nor want. And, so today, I hear
The Oceans; restless roar borne by the stormy wind,
The impetuous torrent's dance riotous and swift and blind
Disdaining walls of rock: the voice of thunder deep
Awakening with its giant call the clouds of Sleep.
Amid this song of triumph vast encircling me,
Rabindranth, O Aurobindo, bows to thee!

CHRONOLOGY

1872	August 15, Aurobindo Ackroyd Ghose born in Calcutta
1879	Taken to England
1884	Admitted to St Paul's School, London
1889	Passes Matriculation from St Paul's
1890	Admitted as a probationer to the Indian Civil Service; Joins King's College, Cambridge, on a scholarship
1892	Passes the first part of the Classical Tripos; Passes the Indian Civil Service Final Examination; Disqualified from the Indian Civil Service
1893	Returns to India, joins Baroda State Service; Contributes articles to *Induprakash*
1901	Marriage to Mrinalini Bose
1905	Writes *Bhawani Mandir;* Vice-Principal, Baroda State College

1906	Writes for *Yugantar;* Starts *Bande Matram;* Indian National Congress splits
1908	Meets Lele; Arrested
1909	Acquited; Starts *Karamyogin*
1910	Leaves Calcutta for Chandarnagore; Arrives in Pondicherry on April 4
1914	First meeting of Sri Aurobindo and The Mother; Publishes *Arya*
1918	Mrinalini Ghose dies
1920	The Mother returns
1921	Last issue *of Arya*
1926	Victory Day
1928	Publication of *The Mother*
1929	Meeting with Rabindranath Tagore
1938	Accident, breaks right leg
1940	Publication of *The Life Divine*
1942	Supports Cripps proposals for Self-Rule
1948	Publication of *The Synthesis of Yoga*
1950	Publication of *Savitri*, Part One; Sri Aurobindo's *mahasamadhi* on December 5

A BIBLIOGRAPHIC NOTE

All books have been published by Sri Aurobindo Ashram, Pondicherry, unless otherwise indicated

A 30-volume edition of *The Sri Aurobindo Birth Centenary Library (SABCL)* was published in 1972. It contained all of Sri Aurobindo's published works. In 1997, on the occasion of Sri Aurobindo's 125th Birth Anniversary, the publication of a new 35-volume scholarly edition under the title *The Collected Works Of Sri Aurobindo* began. It will contain all of Sri Aurobindo's published and unpublished works, with the most authentic version of the texts to-date.

The principal works of Sri Aurobindo are available in separate volumes:

The Life Divine
The Synthesis Of Yoga
Savitri
Essays On The Gita

The Human Cycle

The Foundations Of Indian Culture

Some of these are also available in the form of a CD-ROM.

A number of anthologies of Sri Aurobindo's writings are also available. They are *The Essential Writings Of Sri Aurobindo*(Edited by Peter Heehs, Oxford University Press), *A Sri Aurobindo Anthology*(Edited by Makarand Paranjape, Penguin), and *India's Rebirth* (Mira Aditi, Mysore).

The standard biographies are *Sri Aurobindo: A Biography And A History* by K.R. Srinivas Iyengar (Sri Aurobindo International Centre Of Education, Pondicherry) and *The Life Of Sri Aurobindo* by A.B. Purani. *Mahayogi Sri Aurobindo* is an early biography by R.R. Diwakar (Bharatiya Vidya Bhavan). A short but comprehensive and enlightening study is *Sri Aurobindo: A Brief Biography* by Peter Heehs (Oxford University Press). Sri Aurobindo's autobiographical writings are collected in *On Himself.* Nirodbaran's *Talks with Sri Aurobindo* and *Correspondence With Sri Aurobindo,* and A.B. Purani's *Evening Talks* are valuable. Nirodbaran's experiences as Sri Aurobindo's secretary are recorded in *Twelve Years With Sri Aurobindo.* Wilfred's *The Mother* is a short but useful biography. *The Political Philosophy Of Sri Aurobindo* by

V.P. Varma (Motilal Banarsidas) and *Prophet Of Indian Nationalism* by Karan Singh (Bharatiya Vidya Bhavan) are essential for an understanding of Sri Aurobindo's political life and ideas. *Six Pillars* (Edited by Robert McDermott, Wilson Books) consists of essays on Sri Aurobindo's major works. *The Integral Yoga of Sri Aurobindo* by Rishabchand and *An Introduction To Sri Aurobindo's Philosophy* by Joan Price are also of use. *Sri Aurobindo: The Perfect And The Good* by Robert Minor (Firma KLM) and *The Quest For Political And Spiritual Liberation* by June O'Connor are major studies of Sri Aurobindo's philosophy.

M.P. Pandit's numerous books, of which *Sri Aurobindo, Yoga In Savitri, Sri Aurobindo And His Yoga,* are just a few are the distillation of nearly 50 years study of Sri Aurobindo's life and works.

More information on the life and work of Sri Aurobindo can be obtained from Sri Aurobindo Ashram, Pondicherry.
Books by and on Sri Aurobindo and The Mother can be obtained from SABDA, Sri Aurobindo Ashram, Pondicherry.